Oliver Czarnetta

✹

In Zusammenarbeit mit / in collaboration with:
Kunstverein Siegen e.V.

Verlag der Galerie Epikur Wuppertal

Dorothea Eimert

DAS HAUS IM HAUS IM HAUS …
Neuere Arbeiten von Oliver Czarnetta

Das Haus im Haus, ein weiteres Haus und wiederum ein Haus – man könnte nach diesem Prinzip der ummantelnden Reihung weiter bauen und die Häuser unendlich oft durch ein neues Haus umhüllen. Oliver Czarnetta formt hausähnliche Kästen aus Beton, die sich umeinander staffelnd umhüllen und Schicht auf Schicht größere Dimensionen annehmen. Gegeneinander versetzte Öffnungen ermöglichen dem Betrachter einen begrenzten Blick ins Innere.

Die Skulpturen bauen sich im Schichtensystem auf. Ein ähnliches Prinzip wandte der Künstler für die Skulpturen der früheren Serie, die »Köpfe«, an. Im Jahr 2006 hatte Oliver Czarnetta begonnen, lebensgroße Köpfe in transparentem Harz zu gießen. Es sind glatte Skulpturen, aufgebaut aus bis zu zwanzig gläsernen, nahtlos verschmolzenen Harzlagen. Jede Ebene enthält verschlüsselte Botschaften aus Buchstaben, Wörtern, Zahlenfolgen oder Texte. Sie schwimmen wie Projektionen im fließenden Raum.

Das Prinzip der Schichtungen und des Verbergens ist Grundlage der Philosophie von Oliver Czarnettas künstlerischem Tun – so auch bei den Betonskulpturen »…Haus im Haus im Haus…«. Das Auge des Betrachters zieht durch die eine oder andere Öffnung ein in die Verschachtelungen der etwa 1,5 cm dünnen senkrecht und waagerecht gesetzten Schichten aus Beton. Das Auge tastet sich von einer Wandsperre zur nächsten, dringt tiefer ein ins Labyrinth der Wände, Decken, Fußböden; gelegentlich versperrt eine Treppe den Einblick. Das Auge gleitet zu einer neuen Wandöffnung und entdeckt eine weitere, sie ist geometrisch scharf geschnitten oder das ein oder andere mal wie willkürlich eingebrochen, das Auge wandert tiefer und tiefer in die Hausverschachtelungen bis zum ursprünglichen und kleinsten Haus der gesamten Formation. Hier verbirgt sich die Ur-Idee »Haus«, das Herz der Skulptur.

In der Psychologie steht das Haus für die menschliche Seele. Oliver Czarnettas Hausschachtelungen verstehen sich als

Spectrum, 2011, resin, binoculars, lifesize

Sinnbild des Menschen. Seine Skulpturen können als Persönlichkeiten begriffen werden, die sich entfalten, entwickeln und wachsen. Diesem Grundplan der Natur, des Wachsens in »Ringen«, dieser Aufbau in Schichten unterliegt alles Lebendige, jede Materie, alles Sichtbare und Nicht-Sichtbare, eine Pflanze, ein Baum, ein Stein und auch der Mensch mit seinem physischen Körper, dem Geist und auch der Psyche.

Aus spiritueller Sicht sind dem Menschen sieben Körper zugeordnet, von denen ich nur vier an dieser Stelle nenne: die physische Hülle oder der Nahrungskörper, der Vitalkörper, der lebenswichtige Vorgänge wie Atmung, Kreislauf, Stress regelt, der Geistkörper mit den höheren feinstofflichen Funktionen und dem Wissen des Unterbewusstseins und der Wissenskörper, der klaren Geist, Intuitionen und Emotionen bereithält.

Oliver Czarnetta entwickelt die Häuserskulpturen von innen nach außen, von ganz klein bis ganz groß. Der Betrachter dagegen nimmt die entgegengesetzte Richtung. Er sieht die Haushüllen von außen sich Stufe um Stufe verkleinern bis zu einem zentralen Kern, dem Urhaus. Die Entwicklung des Verschachtelns vollzieht sich demnach in beide Richtungen, von innen nach außen und zugleich von außen nach innen – je nach Blickrichtung und Denkansatz.

Der Mikrokosmos bedingt den Makrokosmos und umgekehrt. Die Skulpturen von Oliver Czarnetta werden in der Regel in Häusern oder Museen ausgestellt und werden somit wiederum von einem Haus umhüllt. Und diese Häuser in unseren Straßen, Dörfern und Städten, diese kleinsten Zellen in der Stadt, reihen sich aneinander, bündeln sich, werden ihrerseits von Atmosphäre und dem gesamten Kosmos umhüllt. Die Kohärenz alles Seienden verdeutlicht sich somit in den Skulpturen von Oliver Czarnetta. Alles auf der Welt und im Kosmos ist untereinander vernetzt, bedingt sich gegenseitig, wirkt gegenseitig aufeinander ein, ob wir das wollen oder nicht.

Die frühen Häuserformen von Oliver Czarnetta stellen sich als kleine Betonbehälter vor mit Füßen oder mit Zähnen als Zeichen von Verwurzelung, von Heimatbezogenheit. Es folgten Häuser, deren Aussehen eher an eine Schutzeinrichtung erinnert. Manche Formen schienen Bunker mit Guckschlitzen entlehnt. Manche nannte der Künstler »Erkenntnismaschinen«, weil der Betrachter in sie hineinsehen konnte und im Spiegel ins eigene Auge, in die eigene Nase oder das eigene Kinn sah – aus einer bisher nicht gekannten Perspektive.

Beton ist für Oliver Czarnetta ein »wunderschönes Material. Es hat«, so der Künstler, »den Hauch von Überdauern, von Ewigem«. Beton ist eine Mischung aus Zement und Zuschlagstoffen wie Kies oder Sand. »Die Einschlüsse machen das Material sehr lebendig und zudem optisch sehr haptisch«. Technisch/handwerklich entsteht das Kunstwerk in einer Art von Wachsausschmelzverfahren. Am Beginn der Arbeit steht ein modellierter Kern aus Styrodur, der mit Wachs ummantelt wird. Auf diese Weise wird Schicht um Schicht aufgebaut. Im Ofen schmilzt das Wachs, so dass Hohlräume entstehen. »In diesen Hohlräumen, die ich mit Beton ausgieße, entsteht das eigentliche Kunstwerk. Die ganze Zeit arbeite ich mit diesen Hohlräumen, also mit der Negativform, mit dem Nichts. Das Nichts dokumentiere ich in Beton. Das ist ein äußerst spannender Prozess.«

Häuser sind auch Schutzeinrichtungen. Die lateinische Wortwurzel für Haus ist »domus«, damit verwandt ist »domestizieren«, das Zähmen der Natur. Das Haus dient dem Schutz und der Erhaltung des Körpers, ist sicherer Ort für die wichtigsten Dinge, ist bergende Hülle gegen Witterung und vor Einblicken und dem Eingriff anderer. Jeder Raum, jedes Haus hat aufgrund seiner besonderen Form, seiner Öffnungen und der Ausgestaltung eine eigene Schwingung, eine eigene Atmosphäre.

Das geschlossene Haus ist ein geschütztes Haus, ein aufgeschnittenes oder aufgebrochenes Haus wie bei Oliver Czarnetta gibt sein Innenleben schutzlos preis. Doch in Czarnettas Häuser kann der Betrachter nicht wirklich schauen. Es gibt zwar Öffnungen. Diese fungieren auch als Filter zwischen Außen und Innen. Hier fließt spürbar Energie gebündelt ein und aus. Diese Öffnungen aber sind stets versetzt zueinander gestellt, so gibt es zwar Durchblicke und Reinblicke, aber Verwinkelungen lassen die volle Einsicht nicht zu. So bleibt mancher Winkel im Verborgenen. Die verborgene Ecke wird zur »Hinterecke« wie wir sie aus manchen Gebetshäusern und Kirchen kennen. Es waren und sind Orte, an denen ein Heiligtum vor fremden Blicken geschützt ist. Das Verbergen erhält hier bei Oliver Czarnetta eine geheimnisvolle Dimension, ähnlich den sogenannten »Hinterecken«, denen unerklärliche Macht und Kraft innewohnt.

Dorothea Eimert

THE HOUSE IN THE HOUSE IN THE HOUSE …
Recent work by Oliver Czarnetta

The house in a house, another house still and a house again – the principle of serial encapsulation could be extended ad infinitum and house constructed upon house as often as whim would have it so. Oliver Czarnetta moulds house-like boxes of concrete which, staggered about and enveloping each other, take on dimensions that grow layer by layer. Apertures again staggered in relation to each other allow the visitor a restricted view into the interior.

The sculptures are built up in a layer system – a principle the artist applied in a similar way in the sculptures of the earlier cycle of ›Heads‹ (Köpfe). In 2006, he had begun to cast life-size heads in transparent resin. These are smooth sculptures, built up out of up to seven glassy layers of resin fused together with no visible join. Each layer contains encoded messages composed of letters, words, series of numbers or texts. Like projected images they drift through the fluid space.

The principle of stratifying and concealing is the foundation of Oliver Czarnetta's artistic activity, and so, consistently, of the concrete sculptures »… Haus im Haus im Haus …«. The viewer's eye makes its way through one opening or the other into the nest system of layers of concrete some one-and-a-half centimetres thin and set in place vertically and horizontally. The eye gropes its way from one barring wall to the next, penetrating further into the labyrinth of walls, ceilings, floors; occasionally a flight of steps bars the view in. The eye slips to a new wall opening and discovers another – cut with geometric precision, or, now and again, as if wilfully broken through. The eye wanders ever deeper into the nested houses, down to the original and smallest house of the entire formation. This is where the very first ›house‹ idea is hidden, the heart of the sculpture.

In psychology, the house stands for the human soul. Oliver Czarnetta's nests of houses are conceived as a symbol of humankind. His sculptures can be taken as personalities in the process of unfolding, in development and growth. To this matrix of nature, of growth in ›rings‹, this construction in layers, all

Home, 2008, resin, pigtooth, plaster, height 10 cm

that is alive is subject, all matter, all that is visible and not visible, a plant, a tree, a stone and human beings likewise with their physical body, with spirit, psyche, and all.

From a spiritual perspective, there are to human beings seven bodies or sheaths. Here I would mention only four of these attributions, namely the physical or food-apparent sheath, the husk or vital body which governs crucial processes such as breathing and circulation and which regulates stress; the spiritual sheath, which, with its higher fine or subtle material functions and the knowledge of the subconscious and the bodies of knowledge, furnishes a lucid spirit, intuitions and emotions.

Oliver Czarnetta develops his house sculptures from the inside outward, from minuscule to very, very big. By contrast, the beholder takes a path in the opposite direction – seeing the sheaths or husks of the houses diminishing from outside step by step all the way to a central core at last, the primordial house. The development of the nesting process thus ensues in both directions, from the inside out and at the same time from the outside in – all depending on one's angle of vision and the general direction of one's thinking at the time.

The microcosm determines the macrocosm, and vice-versa. Oliver Czarnetta's sculptures are generally exhibited in houses or museums, and so are enveloped in turn by a house; and these houses in our streets, villages and cities, these smallest cells in the city, coalesce in rows or clusters only to be enveloped again by atmosphere and by the entire cosmos. The coherence of all being thus becomes manifest in Czarnetta's sculptures. All that inhabits the world or the cosmos is interlinked and interdependent, of reciprocal influence whether we wish it so or not.

Czarnetta's early house works came as little vessels of concrete with feet or teeth to tell of their rootedness, of their connection to a home. Next came houses whose appearance was more reminiscent of a protective device or shelter. Some forms seemed to be borrowed from bunkers with observation slits and some the artist called »Erkenntnismaschinen« or ›knowledge machines‹ because viewers could look inside them and see their own eye in a mirror, could find themselves facing their own nose or chin – from a perspective they had not known before.

For Oliver Czarnetta, concrete is a ›wonderful material. It has,‹ he says, ›the touch of enduring, of the eternal.‹ Concrete is a mixture of cement and aggregates such as gravel or sand. ›The inclusions very much bring the material to life and make it optically very tangible, too.‹ In terms of the craft technique, the work of art comes about in a kind of lost wax process. The point of departure is a modelled core of hard polystyrene foam, which is given a coat of wax. In this way, layer is built upon layer. In the kiln the wax melts, so that cavities are created. ›In these cavities, which I cast in concrete, is where the work of art properly speaking is made. It is these concave spaces, i.e. the negative forms, that I work with, all the time – that is, with nothing. I record the void in concrete. That's an extremely exciting process.‹

Houses, too, are a means of protection – a shelter. The Latin root of the word house is »domus«, and the term »domestication« is related to it: the taming of nature. The house serves as protection and to preserve the body. It is a secure place for the most vital things; it is a sheltering mantle against the weather and against peering eyes and outside interference. Every room and every house, owing to its special shape, its openings and the overall and detail design, has a vibration of its own, its own atmosphere.

A house shut is a protected house, a house which has been cut (or broken) open like Czarnetta's, renders up its inner soul, defenceless. Yet Czarnetta's houses do not really allow the viewer to look in. There are openings; but they function equally as filters between outside and in. Tangibly, packed energy flows in and out of these apertures; but these openings are always staggered in relation to each other, so that while there are views through and in, the intricate turns and angles admit no full interior view. Thence many a nook remains concealed. The hidden spot becomes the ›farthest recess‹ familiar to us from some houses of prayer and churches. These were and are places where a shrine or sacred relic is kept safe from non-initiate eyes. Here, in the work of Oliver Czarnetta, the act of concealing obtains a mysterious dimension much as those ›recesses‹ do with their indwelling might and force.

Single interior – View of the double chin II, 2006, concrete, mirror, 30 × 40 × 28 cm

Plates

Nº 1

Nº 9

N°7

Nº 4

Nº 5

N° 15

Nº 3

Nº 16

Nº 20

Nº 22

Oliver Czarnetta

Aachen / Aix-la-Chapelle
1966   born at Birkesdorf, Düren, Germany
1992   Final examination as apprentice stonemason.
         Working since then as an independent artist.
1993 – 2004 Studies: History of Art, Philosophy; PhD.
2007 – 2009 Artistic member of staff at Institut für Kunstwissenschaft / Institute of Art History and Theory at University of Koblenz

Selected Exhibitions
2011   One-man show, Kunstverein Siegen, Siegen
2009   One-man show, Kunstverein Eschweiler
         One-man show, Galerie Teapot, Cologne
2008   Participation in »Stadt als Urbild«, Galerie Netuschil, Darmstadt
         One-man show at Neue Galerie Kloster Bronnbach, Bronnbach
2007   Work included at Museum Schwarzenberg
2006   One-man show, Galerie Lutz Rohs, Düren
         One-man show, Galerie 23m², Aachen
2005   »Dürener Kulturtage« arts festival, Schloss Burgau (with Prof. Walter Cüppers et al.)
         One-man show at Schloss Neersen, Temporäre Galerie der Stadt Neersen
         Kunstbunker im Nordpark, Mönchengladbach (with Prof. Thomas Virnich et al.)
2004   Participating artist at Museum Hollfeld, Hollfeld
         Work on sculpture representing the Cathedral at Aachen for the UNESCO exhibition at New York
2003   Participating artist at »Kunstbombe«, Herne
         One-man show, Galerie Downtoart, Ghent
2002   Gallery of Fine Art, Luxembourg
2001   Work shown at »International Sculptors Exhibition«, National Museum of Contemporary Art, Seoul / Korea
2000   One-man show, Burg Stolberg, Stolberg

Plates

Nº 1	Haus im Haus im Haus 1	2010	Beton/concrete	40 × 30 × 40 cm
Nº 2	Haus im Haus im Haus 2	2010	Beton/concrete	40 × 30 × 40 cm
Nº 3	Haus im Haus im Haus 3	2010	Beton/concrete	53 × 55 × 50 cm
Nº 4	Haus im Haus im Haus 4	2010	Beton/concrete	45 × 39 × 70 cm
Nº 5	Haus im Haus im Haus 5	2010	Beton/concrete	28 × 24 × 27 cm
Nº 6	Haus im Haus im Haus 6	2010	Beton/concrete	28 × 24 × 27 cm
Nº 7	Haus im Haus im Haus 7	2010	Beton/concrete	47 × 40 × 40 cm
Nº 8	Haus im Haus im Haus 8	2010	Beton/concrete	34 × 31 × 34 cm
Nº 9	Haus im Haus im Haus 9	2010	Beton/concrete	38 × 30 × 38 cm
Nº 10	Haus im Haus im Haus 10	2010	Beton/concrete	37 × 31 × 33 cm
Nº 11	Haus im Haus im Haus 11	2010	Beton/concrete	40 × 31 × 34 cm
Nº 12	Haus im Haus im Haus 12	2010	Beton/concrete	38 × 33 × 34,5 cm
Nº 13	Haus im Haus im Haus 13	2010	Beton/concrete	39 × 26 × 38 cm
Nº 14	Haus im Haus im Haus 14	2010	Beton/concrete	38 × 30 × 36,5 cm
Nº 15	Haus im Haus im Haus 15	2010	Beton/concrete	49 × 51 × 45 cm
Nº 16	Haus im Haus im Haus 16	2010	Beton/concrete	36 × 31 × 34 cm
Nº 17	Haus im Haus im Haus 17	2010	Beton/concrete	33 × 28 × 38 cm
Nº 18	Haus im Haus im Haus 18	2010	Beton/concrete	40 × 33 × 40 cm
Nº 19	Haus im Haus im Haus 19	2010	Beton/concrete	39 × 24 × 33 cm
Nº 20	Haus im Haus im Haus 20	2010	Beton/concrete	30 × 30 × 36 cm
Nº 21	Haus im Haus im Haus 21	2010	Beton/concrete	34 × 34 × 41 cm
Nº 22	Haus im Haus im Haus 22	2010	Beton/concrete	36 × 33 × 30 cm

Colofon

Publikation zur Ausstellung / publication accompanying the exhibition:
Oliver Czarnetta ... HAUS IM HAUS IM HAUS ...
March 18 – April 25, 2011, Kunstverein Siegen e.V.,
Ausstellungsforum des Siegerlandmuseums, Oranienstr. 9, 57072 Siegen

Mit freundlicher Unterstützung von / kindly supported by:
Galerie am Elisengarten, Aachen | Galerie Epikur, Wuppertal | Galerie Teapot, Köln |
Architekturwerkstatt Infra Plan GmbH, Siegen | Alexander Kölsch, Dipl.-Ing. Architekt,
Siegen | Moerschel Architekturkontor, Siegen | Ursula Wagener, Designer grad. Innen-
architektur, Siegen

Herausgeber / Editors: Verlag der Galerie Epikur Wuppertal und Oliver Czarnetta
Text / Essay: Dorothea Eimert, ehem. Direktorin Leopold-Hoesch-Museum Düren
Übersetzung / Translation: Stephen Reader
Fotografie / Photography: Kirstin Römer, Philipp Althoff, Oliver Czarnetta
Lithografie & Gestaltung / Lithography & Design: Marco Lietz
Druck / Printing: Druckservice HP Nacke KG, Wuppertal
Schriften / Fonts: Bello Script, URW Egyptienne
Papier / Paper: GardaPat 13 Kiara, 150 g

© 2011 Oliver Czarnetta, Dorothea Eimert & Verlag der Galerie Epikur Wuppertal
ISBN 978-3-925489-89-1

Verlag der Galerie Epikur Wuppertal
HansPeter Nacke
Friedrich-Ebert-Straße 152
42117 Wuppertal
www.galerie-epikur.de
info@galerie-epikur.de